Your Voice Is a **Warrior's War Trumpet** Full of Fire.™

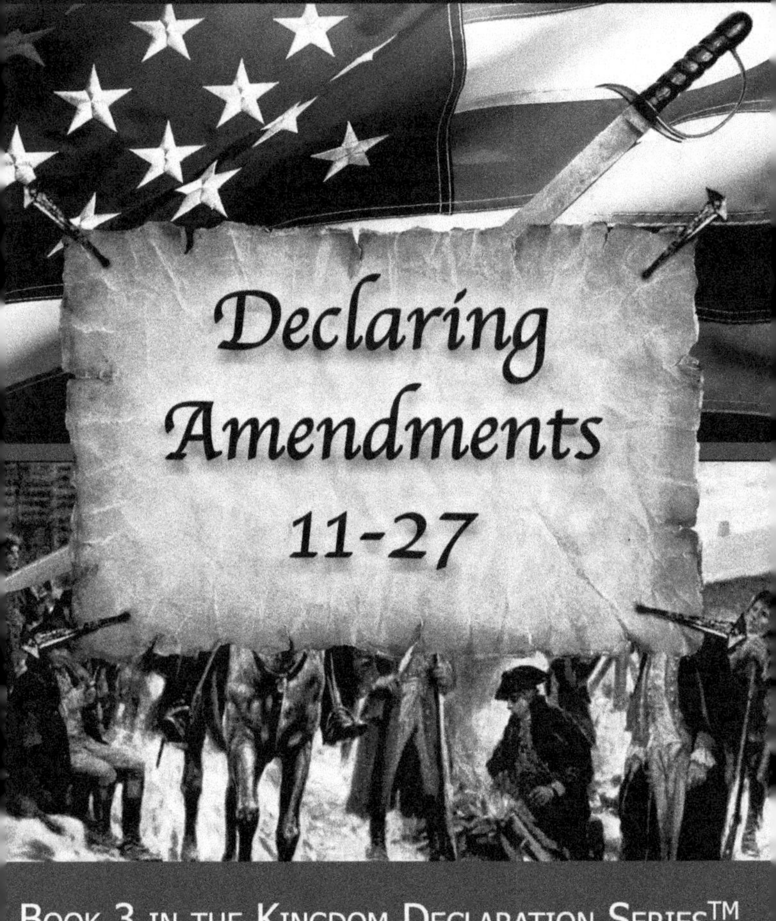

Declaring Amendments 11-27

Book 3 in the Kingdom Declaration Series™

Nathan Daniel Pietsch

Prayer Video :: www.BattleAxeTV.com

Book 3 in the *Kingdom Declaration Series*™
Declaring Amendments 11-27

Copyright © 2023 by All Sufficient God Church and Nathan D. Pietsch
All rights reserved.

ISBN-13: 978-0-9765775-3-9

Editor: Lauri Homestead

NOTICE OF RIGHTS
This book is protected under the copyright laws of the United States of America and may not be copied or reprinted for commercial gain or profit. Any quotations or excepts taken from this book must receive prior written consent from All Sufficient God Church and/or Nathan D. Pietsch.

NOTICE OF LIABILITIES
The information in this book is distributed on an "as is" basis without warranty. While every precaution has been taken in the preparation of this book, neither the publisher, author, nor ministry shall have any liability to any person or entity with respect to any loss or damage caused or alleged to be caused directly or indirectly by the information contained in this book. All Sufficient God Church nor Nathan D. Pietsch assume any liability or responsibility for the use or misuse of this book.

BIBLICAL REFERENCES
All Scriptural references are taken from the New King James Version (NKJV) of the Bible unless otherwise mentioned.

New King James Version (NKJV)
Copyright © 1982 by Thomas Nelson, Inc.

PURCHASE INFORMATION
Declaring Amendments 11-27 is available at special discount rates for bulk purchase. To arrange bulk purchase for sales promotions, premiums, or fundraisers, please contact All Sufficient God Church at: www.AllSufficientGod.org

LEARN MORE OR SCHEDULE NATHAN D. PIETSCH FOR SPEAKING ENGAGEMENTS
To learn more about All Sufficient God Church and/or to schedule Nathan D. Pietsch for speaking engagements, please contact us at:
www.AllSufficientGod.org.

DEDICATION

I would like to dedicate Book 3 in the *Kingdom Declaration Series™: Declaring Amendments 11-27* to my Heavenly Father, my Lord and Savior Jesus Christ, and the Holy Spirit. Everything else is insignificant in comparison to Them.

Acknowledgments

I would like to thank my bride, Dawn, for letting me take the time to write this book. She has been faithful to follow me on this grand adventure with the Lord.

I also want to thank the multitudes of people who have helped me and Dawn with our ministry call.

Jon Courson (Applegate Christian Fellowship)

Kristina Waggoner

Angelo, Andrea, Adam, and Aaron LiVecchi (We See Jesus Ministries, WeSeeJesusMinistries.com)

Alan and Lisa Gluck

Bill and Carol Doyel (Living Better 50, LivingBetter50.com)

Francisco and Carla Reyes (3rd Watch Ministries, 3rdWatchMinistries.com)

Roy and Lorelei Harris (Whirlwind Ministries International)

Sherry Haydel (Sherry Haydel Limited, SherryHaydelLtd.com)

Uzoma Kingsley Akanador and Regina Bianca George (Worphan Charity Organization)

Kathleen Krohn

Myron and Lorie Ace

Rich, Kelley, and Kallee Salber

Bill and Diane Squire

Sharon Lawler

Joe and Jamie Martin

Will and Pam Abbott

Lawrence and Lindsay Elliott

Pastors Frank and Parris Bailey (Victory Church, VictoryChurchNola.com)

Jeremiah Omoto Fufeyin (Christ Mercyland Deliverance Ministry, ChristMercyland.org)

Clint and Faye Pietsch.

Contents

PREFACE — PAGE 17

The U.S. Constitution (17)
The Bill of Rights (18)
Amendments 11-27 (18)

INTRODUCTION — PAGE 21

How to Use This Book (25)
    Original Amendment Transcription (25)
    21st Century Modern Language (25)
    Kingdom Declarations™ (26)

AMENDMENTS 11-27 — PAGE 28

The Eleventh Amendment (29)
    Original Amendment Transcription (30)
    21st Century Modern Language (30)
    Kingdom Declaration™ (31)
The Twelfth Amendment (33)
    Original Amendment Transcription (34)
    21st Century Modern Language (36)
    Kingdom Declaration™ (38)

The Thirteenth Amendment (45)
        Original Amendment Transcription (46)
        21st Century Modern Language (46)
        Kingdom Declaration™ (47)

The Fourteenth Amendment (49)
        Original Amendment Transcription (50)
        21st Century Modern Language (52)
        Kingdom Declaration™ (54)

The Fifteenth Amendment (59)
        Original Amendment Transcription (60)
        21st Century Modern Language (60)
        Kingdom Declaration™ (61)

The Sixteenth Amendment (63)
        Original Amendment Transcription (64)
        21st Century Modern Language (64)
        Kingdom Declaration™ (64)

The Seventeenth Amendment (67)
        Original Amendment Transcription (68)
        21st Century Modern Language (69)
        Kingdom Declaration™ (70)

The Eighteenth Amendment (73)
        Original Amendment Transcription (74)
        21st Century Modern Language (75)
        Kingdom Declaration™ (75)

The Nineteenth Amendment (77)
        Original Amendment Transcription (78)
        21st Century Modern Language (78)
        Kingdom Declaration™ (79)

The Twentieth Amendment (81)
        Original Amendment Transcription (82)
        21st Century Modern Language (84)
        Kingdom Declaration™ (86)

The Twenty-first Amendment (91)
        Original Amendment Transcription (92)
        21st Century Modern Language (93)
        Kingdom Declaration™ (93)

The Twenty-second Amendment (97)
        Original Amendment Transcription (98)
        21st Century Modern Language (99)
        Kingdom Declaration™ (100)

The Twenty-third Amendment (103)
        Original Amendment Transcription (104)
        21st Century Modern Language (105)
        Kingdom Declaration™ (105)

The Twenty-fourth Amendment (109)
        Original Amendment Transcription (110)
        21st Century Modern Language (110)
        Kingdom Declaration™ (111)

The Twenty-fifth Amendment (113)
        Original Amendment Transcription (114)
        21st Century Modern Language (116)
        Kingdom Declaration™ (118)

The Twenty-sixth Amendment (123)
        Original Amendment Transcription (124)
        21st Century Modern Language (124)
        Kingdom Declaration™ (125)

The Twenty-seventh Amendment (127)
        Original Amendment Transcription (128)
        21st Century Modern Language (128)
        Kingdom Declaration™ (128)

ABOUT NATHAN PIETSCH	PAGE 130
ADDITIONAL RESOURCES	PAGE 132
ADDITIONAL BOOKS	PAGE 133
CONNECT WITH NATHAN	PAGE 135
SOW INTO THIS MINISTRY	PAGE 136
SCHEDULE NATHAN	PAGE 137
FOREFATHERS' BLOOD	PAGE 138
GET RIGHT WITH GOD	PAGE 140

Your Voice Is a

Full of Fire.

Preface

THE U.S. CONSTITUTION

Outside of the Holy Bible, the U.S. Constitution is the supreme law of the United States of America. It was created on September 17, 1787. The opening words of the U.S. Constitution state:

"We the People of the United States, in Order to form a more perfect Union, establish Justice, insure domestic Tranquility, provide for the common defense, promote the general Welfare, and secure the Blessings of Liberty to ourselves and our Posterity, do ordain and establish this Constitution for the United States of America."

In this book, we will not talk much about the U.S. Constitution. The emphasis is on Amendments 11-27. To learn more about the Constitution, read Book 1 in the *Kingdom Declaration Series™: Declaring the U.S. Constitution*.

THE BILL OF RIGHTS

The U.S. Constitution has been amended or modified in order to make a correction or improvement 27 times. The first 10 Amendments are known as the Bill of Rights. These Rights offer specific protections of individual liberty and justice. They guarantee the rights of freedom of speech, press, and religion. They also place restrictions on the powers of government within the U.S. states.

Book 2 in the *Kingdom Declaration Series™: Declaring the Bill of Rights*, examines the first ten Amendments to the U.S. Constitution. If you are interested in purchasing this book, or would like to learn more, please visit: www.AllSufficientGod.org.

AMENDMENTS 11-27

The bulk of the remaining 17 Amendments expand individual civil rights protections. They also address issues related to federal authority or modify government processes and procedures.

Amendments 11-27 span the course of three centuries. Amendment 11 was ratified, or made official, on February 7, 1795. The 27th Amendment was ratified on May 7, 1992.

As you read on, you will declare each of these Amendments with power and authority. You can also pray along with Nathan in a video on www.BattleAxeTV.com.

Introduction

We are living in uncertain times. Injustice seems to be prevailing. Parents are being bullied and sued for asking the educational board in their school district what their children are being taught. Law-abiding gun owners are termed evil for standing on their right to own a firearm. Villains are being heralded as heroes and heroes villains.

Leftist liberals want to abolish the U.S. Constitution. They claim it is nothing but a White Supremacist document that holds no relevance for today.

The United States is under attack. Its founding documents are being scrutinized. The constitutional federal republic is being threatened. Those who love America are at risk.

The battle against good and evil, moral and immoral, light and dark, right and wrong continues to rage. In recent days the intensity of evil has heightened. However, we shouldn't be surprised at this. Jesus warned us about such situations in John 16:1-4 when He said:

> [1] *"These things I have spoken to you, that you should not be made to stumble.* [2] *They will put you out of the synagogues; yes, the time is coming that whoever kills you will think that he offers God service.* [3] *And these things they will do to you because they have not known the Father nor Me.* [4] *But these things I have told you, that when the time comes, you may remember that I told you of them."*

We are in a spiritual war. The Apostle Paul wrote in Ephesians 6:12:

> [12] *For we do not wrestle against flesh and blood, but against principalities, against powers, against the rulers of the darkness of this age, against spiritual hosts of wickedness in the heavenly places.*

The true enemy against our freedoms, rights, nation, and lives are not people per se, but satanic entities controlling them. Fortunately, the Heavenly Father, Jesus, and Holy Spirit has given His children the ability to fight back in the spirit. We are told in 2 Corinthians 10:4:

> ⁴ *For the weapons of our warfare are not carnal but mighty in God for pulling down strongholds.*

As followers of Jesus Christ we have been empowered to pull down satanic strongholds warring against us. One way to pull down these strongholds, and perhaps the most powerful weapon of war the Lord has given you, is your voice. Your voice is a *Warrior's War Trumpet™* that destroys the works of the devil. Your voice sounds the alarm of danger. Your voice rallies the troops. Your voice carries fire. Your voice holds life and death. The Bible tells us in Proverbs 18:21:

> ²¹ *Death and life are in the power of the tongue, And those who love it will eat its fruit.*

There is a verse in Job that emphasizes the power of your words and declarations. The Bible says in Job 22:28a-b:

> ²⁸ *You [people] will also declare a thing, And it will be established for you...*

This is the significance of the *Kingdom Declaration Series™*. As you speak forth the declarations in this book, you will be co-creating and establishing dominion with God. As you declare, let God put His holy fire in your mouth. Let your words be proclaimed with power and authority. The Book of James 5:16d says:

> ¹⁶ᵈ *...The effective, fervent prayer of a righteous man avails much.*

Introduction -25-

How to Use This Book

All of the Amendments in this book are broken into three different sections.

Original Amendment Transcription

First, you will see the original transcription of the Amendments. It is transcribed with the word usage and spelling as the original text. You will find grammatical variances in comparison to our current language.

21st Century Modern Language

Second, you will see the Amendments written in 21st century modern language. This will make it easier for you to understand the meaning of the Amendment.

Kingdom Declarations™

Third, you will see the Amendment broken down into a *Kingdom Declaration*™. In this section you will speak forth the prayers written for you. Each declaration will be proclaimed out loud. Verbalize the words with vigor in the name of Jesus Christ. If you like, you can follow along with Nathan as he leads you through the prayers in a video.

Please visit: www.BattleAxeTV.com.

Amendments 11-27

The 11th Amendment

THE ELEVENTH AMENDMENT

ORIGINAL AMENDMENT TRANSCRIPTION

The Judicial power of the United States shall not be construed to extend to any suit in law or equity, commenced or prosecuted against one of the United States by Citizens of another State, or by Citizens or Subjects of any Foreign State.

21st CENTURY MODERN LANGUAGE

If a person of one U.S. State is in a court case with another person from a different state, the national U.S. courts do not have the power to make decisions in these types of cases. In addition, the national U.S. courts do not have the power to make decisions in cases between a U.S. State or a person from a foreign country.

KINGDOM DECLARATION™

In the name of Jesus Christ, on behalf of the United States of America, I declare if a person of one U.S. State is in a court case with another person from a different state, the national U.S. courts do not have the power to make decisions in these types of cases.

In the name of Jesus Christ, on behalf of the United States of America, I declare the national U.S. courts do not have the power to make decisions in cases between a U.S. State or a person from a foreign country.

The 12th Amendment

33

THE TWELFTH AMENDMENT

ORIGINAL AMENDMENT TRANSCRIPTION

The Electors shall meet in their respective states, and vote by ballot for President and Vice-President, one of whom, at least, shall not be an inhabitant of the same state with themselves; they shall name in their ballots the person voted for as President, and in distinct ballots the person voted for as Vice-President, and they shall make distinct lists of all persons voted for as President, and of all persons voted for as Vice-President and of the number of votes for each, which lists they shall sign and certify, and transmit sealed to the seat of the government of the United States, directed to the President of the Senate;

The President of the Senate shall, in the presence of the Senate and House of Representatives, open all the certificates and the votes shall then be counted;

The person having the greatest Number of votes for President, shall be the President, if such number be a majority of the whole number of Electors appointed; and if no person have such majority, then from the persons having the highest numbers not exceeding three on the list of those voted for as President, the House of Representatives shall choose immediately, by ballot, the President. But in choosing the President, the votes shall be taken by states, the representation from each state having one vote; a quorum for this purpose shall consist of a member or members from two-thirds of the states, and a majority of all the states shall be necessary to a choice. And if the House of Representatives shall not choose a President whenever the right of choice shall devolve upon them, before the fourth day of March next following, then the Vice-President shall act as President, as in the case of the death or other constitutional disability of the President.

    The person having the greatest number of votes as Vice-President, shall be the Vice-President, if such number be a majority of the whole number of Electors appointed, and if no person have a majority, then from the two highest numbers on the list, the Senate shall choose the Vice-President; a quorum for the purpose shall consist of two-thirds of the whole number of Senators, and a majority of the whole number shall be necessary to a choice. But no person constitutionally ineligible to the office of President shall be eligible to that of Vice-President of the United States.

21ST CENTURY MODERN LANGUAGE

The electors in each U.S. State shall meet in their own states to place a ballot vote for the U.S. President and Vice President. The two candidates are prohibited from being from the same U.S. State. The electors will first vote for the U.S. President. Then in another ballot, the electors will vote for the U.S. Vice President.

The electors will make two separate lists. The first list will be of all the people who received votes to become U.S. President and the number of votes each candidate received. The second list will be of all the people who received votes to become Vice President and the number of votes each candidate received. The electors will then sign, certify, and seal the two lists. The electors will send the two lists to the United States' capitol addressed to the President of the Senate. The President of the Senate shall open all certified mail in a room where the Senators and Representatives are located. The votes shall then be counted with the witnesses in place. The person who received the highest number of votes will become U.S. President, if he received the majority of the votes. If no candidate has received the majority of votes for U.S. President, then the House of Representatives will vote for one of two or three people who did get the most votes. The person who received the most votes from the House of Representatives will become the U.S. President. Each U.S. State will get one vote and must have members present from two thirds of the states. A majority of all the U.S. States must be present to elect the U.S. President.

      If the House of Representatives fails to elect a President before the next 4th of March, then the Vice President shall act as the U.S. President. This would be the same situation regarding the death or disability of the President. The individual who received the majority of votes for Vice President will become the U.S. Vice President. In the event that nobody received the majority of the elector's votes, then the Senate will choose the Vice President from the two people who received the most votes. In order for the Vice President to be chosen, two thirds of all the Senators must be in attendance. For the Vice President to be chosen, a majority of all the Senators is required. A person who does not meet the qualifications to become U.S. President under the regulations of the Constitution is not eligible to become Vice President either.

KINGDOM DECLARATION™

In the name of Jesus Christ, on behalf of the United States of America, I declare the electors in each U.S. State shall meet in their own states to place a ballot vote for the U.S. President and Vice President.

In the name of Jesus Christ, on behalf of the United States of America, I declare the two candidates running for President and Vice President are prohibited from being from the same U.S. State.

In the name of Jesus Christ, on behalf of the United States of America, I declare the electors will first vote for the U.S. President.

In the name of Jesus Christ, on behalf of the United States of America, I declare the electors will vote for the U.S. Vice President in another ballot.

In the name of Jesus Christ, on behalf of the United States of America, I declare the electors will make two separate lists.

In the name of Jesus Christ, on behalf of the United States of America, I declare the first list will be of all the people who received votes to become U.S. President and the number of votes each candidate received.

In the name of Jesus Christ, on behalf of the United States of America, I declare the second list will be of all the people who received votes to become Vice President and the number of votes each candidate received.

In the name of Jesus Christ, on behalf of the United States of America, I declare the electors will sign, certify, and seal the two lists.

In the name of Jesus Christ, on behalf of the United States of America, I declare the electors will send the two lists to the United States' capitol addressed to the President of the Senate.

In the name of Jesus Christ, on behalf of the United States of America, I declare the President of the Senate shall open all certified mail in a room where the Senators and Representatives are located.

In the name of Jesus Christ, on behalf of the United States of America, I declare the votes shall be counted with the witnesses in place.

In the name of Jesus Christ, on behalf of the United States of America, I declare the person who received the highest number of votes will become U.S. President, if he received the majority of the votes.

In the name of Jesus Christ, on behalf of the United States of America, I declare if no candidate has received the majority of votes for U.S. President, then the House of Representatives will vote for one of two or three people who did get the most votes.

In the name of Jesus Christ, on behalf of the United States of America, I declare the person who received the most votes from the House of Representatives will become the U.S. President.

In the name of Jesus Christ, on behalf of the United States of America, I declare the members in the House of Representatives will be people God has anointed and ordained.

In the name of Jesus Christ, on behalf of the United States of America, I declare each U.S. State will get one vote and must have members present from two thirds of the states.

In the name of Jesus Christ, on behalf of the United States of America, I declare a majority of all the U.S. States must be present to elect the U.S. President.

In the name of Jesus Christ, on behalf of the United States of America, I declare if the House of Representatives fails to elect a President before the next 4th of March, then the Vice President shall act as the U.S. President.

In the name of Jesus Christ, on behalf of the United States of America, I declare if there is a death or disability of the President, the Vice President will act as President.

In the name of Jesus Christ, on behalf of the United States of America, I declare the individual who received the majority of votes for Vice President will become the U.S. Vice President.

In the name of Jesus Christ, on behalf of the United States of America, I declare in the event that nobody received the majority of the elector's votes, then the Senate will choose the Vice President from the two people who received the most votes.

In the name of Jesus Christ, on behalf of the United States of America, I declare the Senate will be men and women of Godly virtue.

In the name of Jesus Christ, on behalf of the United States of America, I declare for the Vice President to be chosen, two thirds of all the Senators must be in attendance.

In the name of Jesus Christ, on behalf of the United States of America, I declare for the Vice President to be chosen, a majority of all the Senators is required.

In the name of Jesus Christ, on behalf of the United States of America, I declare a person who does not meet the qualifications to become U.S. President under the regulations of the Constitution is not eligible to become Vice President.

In the name of Jesus Christ, on behalf of the United States of America, I declare honest, true, and fair elections be made.

In the name of Jesus Christ, on behalf of the United States of America, I declare the U.S. President and Vice President will be people after God's own heart.

In the name of Jesus Christ, on behalf of the United States of America, I declare the U.S. President and Vice President will lead the nation towards the Heavenly Father, Jesus, and Holy Spirit.

44

The 13th Amendment

THE THIRTEENTH AMENDMENT

ORIGINAL AMENDMENT TRANSCRIPTION

1. Neither slavery nor involuntary servitude, except as a punishment for crime whereof the party shall have been duly convicted, shall exist within the United States, or any place subject to their jurisdiction.

2. Congress shall have power to enforce this article by appropriate legislation.

21ST CENTURY MODERN LANGUAGE

1. There shall not be any slavery or forced labor in the United States or the territories owned by the United States. However, forced labor can be implemented on a person who has been convicted of a crime by the legal court system.

2. Congress will have the power to enforce this Amendment by making the appropriate laws.

KINGDOM DECLARATION™

In the name of Jesus Christ, on behalf of the United States of America, I declare there shall not be any slavery or forced labor in the United States or the territories owned by the United States.

In the name of Jesus Christ, on behalf of the United States of America, I declare forced labor can be implemented on a person who has been convicted of a crime by the legal court system.

In the name of Jesus Christ, on behalf of the United States of America, I declare all criminals connected to sex slavery, child trafficking, or any form of slavery would be caught and punished to the fullest extent of the law.

In the name of Jesus Christ, on behalf of the United States of America, I declare Congress will have the power to enforce this Amendment by making the appropriate laws.

In the name of Jesus Christ, on behalf of the United States of America, I declare all laws Congress make will reflect the heart of the Heavenly Father, Jesus, and Holy Spirit.

THE FOURTEENTH AMENDMENT

ORIGINAL AMENDMENT TRANSCRIPTION

1. All persons born or naturalized in the United States, and subject to the jurisdiction thereof, are citizens of the United States and of the State wherein they reside. No State shall make or enforce any law which shall abridge the privileges or immunities of citizens of the United States; nor shall any State deprive any person of life, liberty, or property, without due process of law; nor deny to any person within its jurisdiction the equal protection of the laws.

2. Representatives shall be apportioned among the several States according to their respective numbers, counting the whole number of persons in each State, excluding Indians not taxed. But when the right to vote at any election for the choice of electors for President and Vice-President of the United States, Representatives in Congress, the Executive and Judicial officers of a State, or the members of the Legislature thereof, is denied to any of the male inhabitants of such State, being twenty-one years of age, and citizens of the United States, or in any way abridged, except for participation in rebellion, or other

crime, the basis of representation therein shall be reduced in the proportion which the number of such male citizens shall bear to the whole number of male citizens twenty-one years of age in such State.

3. No person shall be a Senator or Representative in Congress, or elector of President and Vice-President, or hold any office, civil or military, under the United States, or under any State, who, having previously taken an oath, as a member of Congress, or as an officer of the United States, or as a member of any State legislature, or as an executive or judicial officer of any State, to support the Constitution of the United States, shall have engaged in insurrection or rebellion against the same, or given aid or comfort to the enemies thereof. But Congress may by a vote of twothirds of each House, remove such disability.

4. The validity of the public debt of the United States, authorized by law, including debts incurred for payment of pensions and bounties for services in suppressing insurrection or rebellion, shall not be questioned. But neither the United States nor any State shall assume or pay any debt or obligation incurred in aid of insurrection or rebellion against the United States, or any claim for the loss or emancipation of any slave; but all such debts,

obligations and claims shall be held illegal and void.

5. The Congress shall have power to enforce, by appropriate legislation, the provisions of this article.

 ## 21st Century Modern Language

1. All people who are born in the United States or go through the process of citizenship who are not citizens of another country are citizens of the United States. They are also citizens of the U.S. State in which they reside.

U.S. States are prohibited from making or enforcing laws which limit the rights of the citizens of the United States.

U.S. States shall not take a person's life, liberty, or property without going through the legal court system.

U.S. States cannot deny any person within its legal authority the equal protection of the laws.

2. The number of representatives each U.S. State shall have will be determined by the population number of that state.

A census shall be taken and people counted to determine how many representatives a U.S. State shall send to Congress. The population total shall not include Native Americans who do not pay taxes. If a U.S. State has limitations on biological males aged 21 or older who can vote for the U.S. President, the Vice President, Representatives in Congress, the governor, and state lawmakers, then that U.S. State shall have a less number of representatives in Congress. The number of representatives will be reduced based on the ratio of biological male citizens with no right to vote to the whole number of biological male citizens 21 years of age or older in that U.S. State. However, do not count biological males 21 years or older who have had their voting rights revoked because they fought against the United States or are guilty of some other crime.

3. People who have taken an oath as a member of Congress, an officer of the United States, as a member of state legislature, an executive officer, or a judicial officer to support the Constitution of the United States, but defaulted and committed insurrection, treason, or rebellion against the United States or aided her enemies, shall lose the right to hold the office of Senator, Representative, or any United States office.

4. The United States will be required to pay all of its debts that were authorized by law. The U.S. will also be liable to pay debts accumulated by pensions, bounties, or services to Armed Forces' members spent to suppress insurrection and rebellion. However, the United States, nor any individual U.S. State, shall pay debt accumulated for the purpose in fighting against the United States in rebellion. The United States will not pay any claims for the freeing of slaves. Any debt of this kind are not legal, therefore not valid.

5. Congress has the power to make laws in order to enforce this Amendment.

Kingdom Declaration™

In the name of Jesus Christ, on behalf of the United States of America, I declare all people who are born in the United States or go through the legal and legitimate process of citizenship who are not citizens of another country are citizens of the United States.

In the name of Jesus Christ, on behalf of the United States of America, I declare people are also citizens of the U.S. State in which they reside.

In the name of Jesus Christ, on behalf of the United States of America, I declare U.S. States are prohibited from making or enforcing laws which limit the rights of the citizens of the United States.

In the name of Jesus Christ, on behalf of the United States of America, I declare U.S. States shall not take a person's life, liberty, or property without going through the legal court system.

In the name of Jesus Christ, on behalf of the United States of America, I declare U.S. States cannot deny any person within its legal authority the equal protection of the laws.

In the name of Jesus Christ, on behalf of the United States of America, I declare the number of representatives each U.S. State shall have will be determined by the population number of that state.

In the name of Jesus Christ, on behalf of the United States of America, I declare a census shall be taken and people counted to determine how many representatives a U.S. State shall send to Congress.

In the name of Jesus Christ, on behalf of the United States of America, I declare biological males 21 years or older who have had their voting rights revoked because they fought against the United States or are guilty of some other crime will not be permitted to vote.

In the name of Jesus Christ, on behalf of the United States of America, I declare people who have taken an oath as a member of Congress, an officer of the United States, as a member of state legislature, an executive officer, or a judicial officer to support the Constitution of the United States, but defaulted and committed insurrection, treason, or rebellion against the United States or aided her enemies, shall lose the right to hold the office of Senator, Representative, or any United States office.

In the name of Jesus Christ, on behalf of the United States of America, I declare the United States will be required to pay all of its debts that were authorized by law.

In the name of Jesus Christ, on behalf of the United States of America, I declare the U.S. will be liable to pay debts accumulated by pensions, bounties, or services to Armed Forces' members spent to suppress insurrection and rebellion.

In the name of Jesus Christ, on behalf of the United States of America, I declare the United States, nor any individual U.S. State, shall pay debt accumulated for the purpose in fighting against the United States in rebellion.

In the name of Jesus Christ, on behalf of the United States of America, I declare Congress has the power to make laws in order to enforce this Amendment.

In the name of Jesus Christ, on behalf of the United States of America, I declare the people in Congress will make laws according to the wisdom of God.

The 15th Amendment

THE FIFTEENTH AMENDMENT

ORIGINAL AMENDMENT TRANSCRIPTION

1. The right of citizens of the United States to vote shall not be denied or abridged by the United States or by any State on account of race, color, or previous condition of servitude.

2. The Congress shall have power to enforce this article by appropriate legislation.

21ST CENTURY MODERN LANGUAGE

1. The citizens of the United States have a right to vote and it shall not be denied by the United States or any U.S. State because of a person's race, color, or previous condition of slavery.

2. Congress has the power to make laws in order to enforce this Amendment.

Kingdom Declaration™

In the name of Jesus Christ, on behalf of the United States of America, I declare the citizens of the United States have a right to vote and it shall not be denied by the United States or any U.S. State because of a person's race, color, or previous condition of slavery.

In the name of Jesus Christ, on behalf of the United States of America, I declare when people vote it will be a fair election and the voters will use Godly discernment and vote for those who adhere to Biblical morals and values.

In the name of Jesus Christ, on behalf of the United States of America, I declare Congress has the power to make laws in order to enforce this Amendment.

In the name of Jesus Christ, on behalf of the United States of America, I declare all laws made by Congress will reflect the Heavenly Father, Jesus, and Holy Spirit.

The 16th Amendment

THE SIXTEENTH AMENDMENT

ORIGINAL AMENDMENT TRANSCRIPTION

The Congress shall have power to lay and collect taxes on incomes, from whatever source derived, without apportionment among the several States, and without regard to any census or enumeration.

21ST CENTURY MODERN LANGUAGE

Congress shall have the power to decide on and collect taxes on income no matter where the income is generated from. This income tax does not depend upon census of people in a U.S. State, nor is it divided among the states.

KINGDOM DECLARATION™

In the name of Jesus Christ, on behalf of the United States of America, I declare Congress shall have the power to decide on and collect taxes on income no matter where the income is generated from.

In the name of Jesus Christ, on behalf of the United States of America, I declare Congress will not collect taxes in unlawful ways.

In the name of Jesus Christ, on behalf of the United States of America, I declare the income tax does not depend upon census of people in a U.S. State, nor is it divided among the states.

In the name of Jesus Christ, on behalf of the United States of America, I declare taxes collected by the U.S. Government would be used for God's divine purposes, and not create undue hardship, or favor certain groups of U.S. Citizens.

THE SEVENTEENTH AMENDMENT

ORIGINAL AMENDMENT TRANSCRIPTION

The Senate of the United States shall be composed of two Senators from each State, elected by the people thereof, for six years; and each Senator shall have one vote. The electors in each State shall have the qualifications requisite for electors of the most numerous branch of the State legislatures.

When vacancies happen in the representation of any State in the Senate, the executive authority of such State shall issue writs of election to fill such vacancies: Provided, That the legislature of any State may empower the executive thereof to make temporary appointments until the people fill the vacancies by election as the legislature may direct. This Amendment shall not be so construed as to affect the election or term of any Senator chosen before it becomes valid as part of the Constitution.

21st Century Modern Language

The Senate of the United States shall be composed of two Senators from each State. The Senators shall be elected by the people and serve a term of six years. Each Senator shall have one vote.

The electors in each U.S. State who vote for the senators shall have the same qualification requirements as the U.S. State has for electors of the most numerous branch of the state legislatures.

When a vacancy arises in the senate due to a senator dying, resigning, or removal, the governor of the U.S. State shall require an election to vote for a new senator. The legislature in a U.S. State may vote to permit the governor to make a temporary appointment until the people vote for a new senator. This Amendment does not impact the term of any U.S. Senator who was in office prior to this Amendment becoming a part of the Constitution.

KINGDOM DECLARATION™

In the name of Jesus Christ, on behalf of the United States of America, I declare the Senate of the United States shall be composed of two Senators from each State.

In the name of Jesus Christ, on behalf of the United States of America, I declare the Senators shall be elected by the people and serve a term of six years.

In the name of Jesus Christ, on behalf of the United States of America, I declare each Senator shall have one vote.

In the name of Jesus Christ, on behalf of the United States of America, I declare senators will have a love for America, the U.S. Constitution, and the Holy Bible.

In the name of Jesus Christ, on behalf of the United States of America, I declare the electors in each U.S. State who vote for the senators shall have the same qualification requirements as the U.S. State has for electors of the most numerous branch of the state legislatures.

In the name of Jesus Christ, on behalf of the United States of America, I declare when a vacancy arises in the senate due to a senator dying, resigning, or removal, the governor of the U.S. State shall require an election to vote for a new senator.

In the name of Jesus Christ, on behalf of the United States of America, I declare the legislature in a U.S. State may vote to permit the governor to make a temporary appointment until the people vote for a new senator.

The 18th Amendment

THE EIGHTEENTH AMENDMENT

Original Amendment Transcription

1. After one year from the ratification of this article the manufacture, sale, or transportation of intoxicating liquors within, the importation thereof into, or the exportation thereof from the United States and all territory subject to the jurisdiction thereof for beverage purposes is hereby prohibited.

2. The Congress and the several States shall have concurrent power to enforce this article by appropriate legislation.

3. This article shall be inoperative unless it shall have been ratified as an Amendment to the Constitution by the legislatures of the several States, as provided in the Constitution, within seven years from the date of the submission hereof to the States by the Congress.

Repealed by the 21st Amendment.

21st Century Modern Language

1. Starting one year after this Amendment is made official (starting January 16, 1920), it shall be illegal to manufacture, sell, transport, import, or export intoxicating liquors and beverages within the United States or any of its territories.

2. Congress and every U.S. State has the power to create laws in order to enforce this Amendment.

3. This Amendment will not be effective unless it is made official by the legislatures of the U.S. States within seven years from the date it was submitted to them by Congress.

The 18th Amendment was repealed by the 21st Amendment.

Kingdom Declaration™

The 18th Amendment was revoked by the 21st Amendment. Please see page 91.

KINGDOM DECLARATION™

In the name of Jesus Christ, on behalf of the United States of America, I declare the right of citizens to vote shall not be denied or limited by the United States or individual U.S. States based upon a person's male, or female, biological birth gender.

In the name of Jesus Christ, on behalf of the United States of America, I declare Congress has the power to make laws in order to enforce this Amendment.

THE TWENTIETH AMENDMENT

ORIGINAL AMENDMENT TRANSCRIPTION

1. The terms of the President and Vice President shall end at noon on the 20th day of January, and the terms of Senators and Representatives at noon on the 3rd day of January, of the years in which such terms would have ended if this article had not been ratified; and the terms of their successors shall then begin.

2. The Congress shall assemble at least once in every year, and such meeting shall begin at noon on the 3d day of January, unless they shall by law appoint a different day.

3. If, at the time fixed for the beginning of the term of the President, the President elect shall have died, the Vice President elect shall become President. If a President shall not have been chosen before the time fixed for the beginning of his term, or if the President elect shall have failed to qualify, then the Vice President elect shall act as President until a President shall have qualified; and the Congress may by law provide for the case wherein neither a President elect nor a Vice President elect shall have qualified, declaring

who shall then act as President, or the manner in which one who is to act shall be selected, and such person shall act accordingly until a President or Vice President shall have qualified.

4. The Congress may by law provide for the case of the death of any of the persons from whom the House of Representatives may choose a President whenever the right of choice shall have devolved upon them, and for the case of the death of any of the persons from whom the Senate may choose a Vice President whenever the right of choice shall have devolved upon them.

5. Sections 1 and 2 shall take effect on the 15th day of October following the ratification of this article.

6. This article shall be inoperative unless it shall have been ratified as an Amendment to the Constitution by the legislatures of three-fourths of the several States within seven years from the date of its submission.

21st Century Modern Language

1. The terms of the U.S. President and Vice President shall end at noon on the 20th day of January in the year in which their term would have ended. Following the end of their terms, the terms of the newly elected U.S. President and Vice President shall begin. The terms of Senators and Representatives shall end at noon on the 3rd day of January in the year in which their term would have ended. Following the end of their terms, the terms of the newly elected Senators and Representatives shall begin.

2. Congress shall gather together at least once per year. The meeting shall begin at noon on the 3rd day of January, unless Congress legally changes it to a different day.

3. If the person elected to become U.S. President dies before the beginning of his term, the Vice President shall become President. If there has not been a U.S. President chosen by the date of January 20th, or if the elected person does not have the qualifications this Constitution requires, then the Vice President shall act as President until a President is qualified. Congress has the power to make a law to determine what happens if both the U.S. President elect and Vice President elect are not

qualified. Congress will determine who shall act as U.S. President or determine how to select a person to act as U.S. President. The person chosen by Congress shall act as U.S. President until a president or vice president does meet the qualifications.

4. If any of the top candidates with the highest votes should die, Congress can make a law stating what will happen in this sort of situation.

Congress may also make a law that states what would happen if any of the people the Senators choose as vice president should die.

5. Sections 1 and 2 will become law on October 15 after this Amendment is made official.

6. In order for this Amendment to be made official, it will take three fourths of the state legislatures to approve it.

If the state legislatures do not make this Amendment official within seven years from the day it is sent to the U.S. States by Congress, then it will not become part of the Constitution.

KINGDOM DECLARATION™

In the name of Jesus Christ, on behalf of the United States of America, I declare the terms of the U.S. President and Vice President shall end at noon on the 20th day of January in the year in which their term would have ended.

In the name of Jesus Christ, on behalf of the United States of America, I declare following the end of the U.S. President and Vice President's terms, the terms of the newly elected U.S. President and Vice President shall begin.

In the name of Jesus Christ, on behalf of the United States of America, I declare the terms of Senators and Representatives shall end at noon on the 3rd day of January in the year in which their term would have ended.

In the name of Jesus Christ, on behalf of the United States of America, I declare following the end of the Senator's and Representative's terms, the terms of the newly elected Senators and Representatives shall begin.

In the name of Jesus Christ, on behalf of the United States of America, I declare Congress shall gather together at least once per year, in Godly unity, to work for the good of the citizens of the United States.

In the name of Jesus Christ, on behalf of the United States of America, I declare the meeting shall begin at noon on the 3rd day of January, unless Congress legally changes it to a different day.

In the name of Jesus Christ, on behalf of the United States of America, I declare if the person elected to become U.S. President dies before the beginning of his term, the Vice President shall become President.

In the name of Jesus Christ, on behalf of the United States of America, I declare if there has not been a U.S. President chosen by the date of January 20th, or if the elected person does not have the qualifications this Constitution requires, then the Vice President shall act as President until a President is qualified.

In the name of Jesus Christ, on behalf of the United States of America, I declare Congress has the power to make a fair and just law to determine what happens if both the U.S. President elect and Vice President elect are not qualified.

In the name of Jesus Christ, on behalf of the United States of America, I declare Congress will determine who shall act as U.S. President or determine how to select a person to act as U.S. President who is Godly and adheres to Biblical standards and values.

In the name of Jesus Christ, on behalf of the United States of America, I declare the person chosen by Congress shall act as U.S. President until a president or vice president does meet the qualifications.

In the name of Jesus Christ, on behalf of the United States of America, I declare if any of the top candidates with the highest votes should die, Congress can make a law stating what will happen in this sort of situation.

In the name of Jesus Christ, on behalf of the United States of America, I declare Congress may make a law that states what would happen if any of the people the Senators choose as vice president should die.

The 21st Amendment

THE TWENTY-FIRST AMENDMENT

ORIGINAL AMENDMENT TRANSCRIPTION

(Amendment 18 Repealed.)

1. The eighteenth article of Amendment to the Constitution of the United States is hereby repealed.

2. The transportation or importation into any State, Territory, or possession of the United States for delivery or use therein of intoxicating liquors, in violation of the laws thereof, is hereby prohibited.

3. The article shall be inoperative unless it shall have been ratified as an Amendment to the Constitution by conventions in the several States, as provided in the Constitution, within seven years from the date of the submission hereof to the States by the Congress.

21st Century Modern Language

(Amendment 18 Repealed.)

1. The eighteenth Amendment to the U.S. Constitution is revoked.

2. People in any U.S. State, territory or possession may transport, import, deliver, or use intoxicating drinks. However, this is not permitted in U.S. States that have laws against it.

3. This Amendment will not take effect until it is made official by conventions in the U.S. States within seven years.

Kingdom Declaration™

In the name of Jesus Christ, on behalf of the United States of America, I declare the eighteenth Amendment to the U.S. Constitution is revoked.

In the name of Jesus Christ, on behalf of the United States of America, I declare people in any U.S. State, territory, or possession may transport, import, deliver, or use intoxicating drinks.

In the name of Jesus Christ, on behalf of the United States of America, I declare that people will not have a desire to overindulge in alcoholic beverages.

In the name of Jesus Christ, on behalf of the United States of America, I declare people who are bound by addictions would be delivered, set free, and restored to an abundant life in the Lord.

The 22nd Amendment

THE TWENTY-SECOND AMENDMENT

ORIGINAL AMENDMENT TRANSCRIPTION

1. No person shall be elected to the office of the President more than twice, and no person who has held the office of President, or acted as President, for more than two years of a term to which some other person was elected President shall be elected to the office of the President more than once. But this Article shall not apply to any person holding the office of President, when this Article was proposed by the Congress, and shall not prevent any person who may be holding the office of President, or acting as President, during the term within which this Article becomes operative from holding the office of President or acting as President during the remainder of such term.

2. This article shall be inoperative unless it shall have been ratified as an Amendment to the Constitution by the legislatures of three-fourths of the several States within seven years from the date of its submission to the States by the Congress.

21st Century Modern Language

1. A person may not be elected as U.S. President more than twice.

If a U.S. Vice President or someone assuming the role as President becomes the U.S. President and serves more than two years as president, then he can only be elected as president one more time.

This Amendment would not stop the person who is president now from being elected president two or more times. (The time this Amendment was made official, Harry S. Truman was the U.S. President.)

2. This Amendment will not become part of the U.S. Constitution unless three fourths of the state legislatures make it official within seven years.

 KINGDOM DECLARATION™

In the name of Jesus Christ, on behalf of the United States of America, I declare a person may not be elected as U.S. President more than twice.

In the name of Jesus Christ, on behalf of the United States of America, I declare if a U.S. Vice President or someone assuming the role as President becomes the U.S. President and serves more than two years as president, then he or she can only be elected as president one more time and that person shall be of Godly and sound, moral character.

The 23rd Amendment

THE TWENTY-THIRD AMENDMENT

 ORIGINAL AMENDMENT
TRANSCRIPTION

1. The District constituting the seat of Government of the United States shall appoint in such manner as the Congress may direct: A number of electors of President and Vice President equal to the whole number of Senators and Representatives in Congress to which the District would be entitled if it were a State, but in no event more than the least populous State; they shall be in addition to those appointed by the States, but they shall be considered, for the purposes of the election of President and Vice President, to be electors appointed by a State; and they shall meet in the District and perform such duties as provided by the twelfth article of Amendment.

2. The Congress shall have power to enforce this article by appropriate legislation.

21st Century Modern Language

1. The District of Columbia (Washington D.C.) shall have the right to choose electors for U.S. President and U.S. Vice President. The District shall have the number of electors they would be entitled to if they were a U.S. State. However, this number shall not be more than the state with the least amount of people. These electors shall be in addition to the electors that the U.S. States have. The electors shall be counted for the purposes of electing a U.S. President and Vice President. Congress shall gather together and vote as explained in the 12th Amendment.

2. Congress shall have the power to make laws in order to enforce this Amendment.

Kingdom Declaration™

In the name of Jesus Christ, on behalf of the United States of America, I declare the District of Columbia shall have the right to choose electors for U.S. President and U.S. Vice President.

In the name of Jesus Christ, on behalf of the United States of America, I declare the District shall have the number of electors they would be entitled to if they were a U.S. State.

In the name of Jesus Christ, on behalf of the United States of America, I declare the number of electors shall not be more than the U.S. State with the least amount of people.

In the name of Jesus Christ, on behalf of the United States of America, I declare the electors shall be in addition to the electors that the U.S. States already have.

In the name of Jesus Christ, on behalf of the United States of America, I declare the electors shall be counted for the purposes of electing a U.S. President and Vice President.

In the name of Jesus Christ, on behalf of the United States of America, I declare the chosen electors will be Godly and have Biblical morals and values.

In the name of Jesus Christ, on behalf of the United States of America, I declare Congress shall gather together and vote as explained in the 12th Amendment.

In the name of Jesus Christ, on behalf of the United States of America, I declare Congress shall have the power to make laws in order to enforce this Amendment.

The 24th Amendment

THE TWENTY-FOURTH AMENDMENT

ORIGINAL AMENDMENT TRANSCRIPTION

1. The right of citizens of the United States to vote in any primary or other election for President or Vice President, for electors for President or Vice President, or for Senator or Representative in Congress, shall not be denied or abridged by the United States or any State by reason of failure to pay any poll tax or other tax.

2. The Congress shall have power to enforce this article by appropriate legislation.

21ST CENTURY MODERN LANGUAGE

1. The United States nor any individual U.S. State shall not make people pay a special or additional tax to vote for U.S. President, Vice President, Senator, Representative in Congress, or any primary election for those officers.

2. Congress shall have the power to make laws in order to enforce this Amendment.

KINGDOM DECLARATION™

In the name of Jesus Christ, on behalf of the United States of America, I declare the United States nor any individual U.S. State shall not make people pay a special or additional tax to vote for U.S. President, Vice President, Senator, Representative in Congress, or any primary election for those officers.

In the name of Jesus Christ, on behalf of the United States of America, I declare Congress shall have the power to make laws in order to enforce this Amendment.

In the name of Jesus Christ, on behalf of the United States of America, I declare the men and women in Congress will be chosen by God.

The 25th Amendment

THE TWENTY-FIFTH AMENDMENT

 ORIGINAL AMENDMENT TRANSCRIPTION

1. In case of the removal of the President from office or of his death or resignation, the Vice President shall become President.

2. Whenever there is a vacancy in the office of the Vice President, the President shall nominate a Vice President who shall take office upon confirmation by a majority vote of both Houses of Congress.

3. Whenever the President transmits to the President pro tempore of the Senate and the Speaker of the House of Representatives his written declaration that he is unable to discharge the powers and duties of his office, and until he transmits to them a written declaration to the contrary, such powers and duties shall be discharged by the Vice President as Acting President.

4. Whenever the Vice President and a majority of either the principal officers of the executive departments or of such other body as Congress may by law provide, transmit to the President pro tempore of the Senate and the Speaker of the House of Representatives their

written declaration that the President is unable to discharge the powers and duties of his office, the Vice President shall immediately assume the powers and duties of the office as Acting President. Thereafter, when the President transmits to the President pro tempore of the Senate and the Speaker of the House of Representatives his written declaration that no inability exists, he shall resume the powers and duties of his office unless the Vice President and a majority of either the principal officers of the executive department or of such other body as Congress may by law provide, transmit within four days to the President pro tempore of the Senate and the Speaker of the House of Representatives their written declaration that the President is unable to discharge the powers and duties of his office. Thereupon Congress shall decide the issue, assembling within forty eight hours for that purpose if not in session. If the Congress, within twenty one days after receipt of the latter written declaration, or, if Congress is not in session, within twenty one days after Congress is required to assemble, determines by two thirds vote of both Houses that the President is unable to discharge the powers and duties of his office, the Vice President shall continue to discharge the same as Acting President; otherwise, the President shall resume the powers and duties of his office.

21ST CENTURY MODERN LANGUAGE

1. If the U.S. President is removed, dies, or resigns from his office, the U.S. Vice President shall become President.

2. If there is a vacancy in the office of the U.S. Vice President, the U.S. President shall nominate a new Vice President. The new Vice President shall take office when the majority of both houses of Congress vote and approve of the President's nomination of the new Vice President.

3. If the U.S. President is not able to perform his job, he may inform the president of the Senate and to the Speaker of the House in a written declaration. The U.S. Vice President will then act as the U.S. President. The Vice President will continue to hold the office of President until the U.S. President sends a written declaration stating he is now able to perform his job.

4. If the U.S. President is unable to perform his job and unable to send a written declaration, the U.S. Vice President and a majority of either the principal officers of the executive department or of such other body as Congress may by law provide a written declaration to the president of the Senate and to the speaker of the House. The letter should

inform the readers that the U.S. President is not capable of performing his job. In this situation, the U.S. Vice President shall act as U.S. President.

If the U.S. President later sends a written declaration to Congress informing them that he is able to carry out his duties, he shall be reinstated to go back to his work.

If the U.S. President is not able to perform his duties, The U.S. Vice President and the other officers will have four days to send a written declaration stating the U.S. President is unable to perform his duties.

Congress will then determine if the U.S. President is able or unable to perform his job. Congress will come together within 48 hours unless they are already in session.

Congress will have up to 21 days to determine if the president is able or unable to perform his job. If Congress decide he cannot accomplish his duties, then the U.S. Vice President shall act as President. If the U.S. President is determined to perform his tasks, he shall go back to his job.

KINGDOM DECLARATION™

In the name of Jesus Christ, on behalf of the United States of America, I declare if the U.S. President is removed, dies, or resigns from his office the U.S. Vice President shall become President.

In the name of Jesus Christ, on behalf of the United States of America, I declare if there is a vacancy in the office of the U.S. Vice President, the U.S. President shall nominate a new Vice President.

In the name of Jesus Christ, on behalf of the United States of America, I declare the new Vice President shall take office when the majority of both houses of Congress vote and approve of the President's nomination of the new Vice President.

In the name of Jesus Christ, on behalf of the United States of America, I declare if the U.S. President is not able to perform his job, he may inform the president of the Senate and to the Speaker of the House in a written declaration.

In the name of Jesus Christ, on behalf of the United States of America, I declare if the U.S. President is unable to perform his job, the U.S. Vice President will then act as the U.S. President.

In the name of Jesus Christ, on behalf of the United States of America, I declare the U.S. President and Vice President will be God-loving and God-fearing men and women from this day forth.

In the name of Jesus Christ, on behalf of the United States of America, I declare the Vice President will continue to hold the office of President until the U.S. President sends a written declaration stating he is able to perform his job.

In the name of Jesus Christ, on behalf of the United States of America, I declare if the U.S. President is unable to perform his job and unable to send a written declaration, the U.S. Vice President and a majority of either the principal officers of the executive department or of such other body as Congress may by law provide, send a written declaration to the president of the Senate and to the speaker of the House.

In the name of Jesus Christ, on behalf of the United States of America, I declare the letter should inform the readers that the U.S. President is not capable of performing his job.

In the name of Jesus Christ, on behalf of the United States of America, I declare if the U.S. President later sends a written declaration to Congress informing them that he is able to carry out his duties, he shall be reinstated to go back to work.

In the name of Jesus Christ, on behalf of the United States of America, I declare if the U.S. President is not able to perform his duties, the U.S. Vice President and the other officers will have four days to send a written declaration stating the U.S. President is unable to perform his duties.

In the name of Jesus Christ, on behalf of the United States of America, I declare Congress will determine if the U.S. President is able or unable to perform his job.

In the name of Jesus Christ, on behalf of the United States of America, I declare Congress will come together within 48 hours unless they are already in session.

In the name of Jesus Christ, on behalf of the United States of America, I declare Congress will have up to 21 days to determine if the president is able or unable to perform his job.

In the name of Jesus Christ, on behalf of the United States of America, I declare if Congress decides he cannot accomplish his duties, then the U.S. Vice President shall act as President.

In the name of Jesus Christ, on behalf of the United States of America, I declare if the U.S. President is determined to perform his tasks, he shall go back to his job.

The 26th Amendment

THE TWENTY-SIXTH AMENDMENT

ORIGINAL AMENDMENT TRANSCRIPTION

1. The right of citizens of the United States, who are eighteen years of age or older, to vote shall not be denied or abridged by the United States or by any State on account of age.

2. The Congress shall have power to enforce this article by appropriate legislation.

21st CENTURY MODERN LANGUAGE

1. United States' citizens who are eighteen years of age or older may not have their right to vote denied because of their age by the United States or any individual U.S. State.

2. Congress shall have power to make laws in order to enforce this Amendment.

KINGDOM DECLARATION™

In the name of Jesus Christ, on behalf of the United States of America, I declare United States' citizens who are eighteen years of age or older may not have their right to vote denied because of their age by the United States or any individual U.S. State.

In the name of Jesus Christ, on behalf of the United States of America, I declare voters will use their voting privilege to appoint Godly men and women to serve in the U.S. Government.

In the name of Jesus Christ, on behalf of the United States of America, I declare Congress shall have power to make fair and just laws in order to enforce this Amendment.

The 27th Amendment

THE TWENTY-SEVENTH AMENDMENT

ORIGINAL AMENDMENT TRANSCRIPTION

No law, varying the compensation for the services of the Senators and Representatives, shall take effect, until an election of Representatives shall have intervened.

21ST CENTURY MODERN LANGUAGE

A law that increases or decreases the financial wages of the Senators and Representatives shall not take effect until after the next election of Representatives.

KINGDOM DECLARATION™

In the name of Jesus Christ, on behalf of the United States of America, I declare a law that increases or decreases the financial wages of the Senators and Representatives shall not take effect until after the next election of Representatives.

In the name of Jesus Christ, on behalf of the United States of America, I declare wage increases and decreases shall be provident according to the financial state of U.S. Citizens, of that time.

About Nathan D. Pietsch

Nathan D. Pietsch was born in Orange County in Fullerton, California,

on September 27th, 1976. As an infant, he was diagnosed with neurofibromatosis, a disease in which tumors attack the nervous system. His doctors anticipated a childhood death. However, the Lord healed Nathan miraculously. He is now a crusade evangelist, preacher, missionary, author, world traveler, and passionate follower of Jesus Christ.

Nathan and his wife, Dawn, travel the world preaching the Good News of Jesus Christ. They have helped bring freedom and transformation to thousands of people bound by the snares of the devil. It is their desire to see captives set free.

As frontline ministers, Nathan and Dawn have a heart for worldwide revival. They partner with churches around the globe to help release a great outpouring of the Holy Spirit in the regions they minister.

As a result, the churches grow in strength and number, unity is established, and the people are released into their life's purpose. Nathan and Dawn help bring renewal through: 1) Gospel crusade evangelism, 2) conducting training and equipping seminars, workshops, and conferences, 3) ministering deliverance and inner healing, and 4) clearing the land and territories of demonic principalities.

Nathan has written numerous books and is the author of the instant classics *The Holiday Devotional Series*. He has also written *Go: Testimonies from the Front Lines*, *Your Royal Destiny: Discovering Your Significance*, and *Decay Castle*.

Additional Resources at BattleAxeTV.com

Battle Axe TV is a media ministry of All Sufficient God Church. The website contains video recordings, audio recordings, and written materials associated with Nathan D. Pietsch and ministry associates. As you watch, listen, or read, expect to receive healing, deliverance, encouragement, revelation, empowerment, equipping, impartation, or salvation.

At Battle Axe TV, we are training warriors for the Great Harvest. Jesus said in John 4:35c (NKJV), *"...Behold, I say to you, lift up your eyes and look at the fields, for they are already white for harvest!"* The great harvest of souls is upon us. God wants to use you to be a "fisher of men" to draw people to Himself. Battle Axe TV can help you prepare for your ministry call.

BATTLEAXETV.COM

WATCH LISTEN READ

Additional Books in the Series

DECLARING THE U.S. CONSTITUTION

We are living in unprecedented times. The rights and freedoms American citizens have enjoyed for generations are under attack. The foundation of our nation is being shaken. The U.S. Constitution has been trampled and spit upon. The blood of our forefathers who won us such privileges is being disgraced.

In *Declaring the U.S. Constitution* we will make *Kingdom Declarations™* that will help expel the darkness and bring transformation to the United States of America.

DECLARING THE BILL OF RIGHTS

America is at war. It is a war against light and dark, good and evil, bondage and freedom. It is a war between God's Kingdom and satan's domain.

In *Declaring the Bill of Rights* we will make *Kingdom Declarations*™ that will help expel the darkness and bring transformation to the United States of America.

DECLARING AMENDMENTS 11-27

Your voice is a *Warrior's War Trumpet*™ that destroys the works of the devil. Your voice sounds the alarm of danger. Your voice rallies the troops. Your voice carries fire. Your voice holds life and death.

In *Declaring Amendments 11-27* we will make *Kingdom Declarations*™ that will help expel the darkness and bring transformation to the United States of America.

Stay tuned for future release dates of additional books in the Kingdom Declaration Series™.

Connect with Nathan D. Pietsch

Battle Axe TV
www.BattleAxeTV.com

All Sufficient God Church
www.AllSufficientGod.org

Frontline Chronicles
www.FrontlineChronicles.com

Holiday Devotionals
www.HolidayDevotionals.com

Facebook
www.facebook.com/nathan.pietsch.9

Youtube
www.youtube.com/@battleaxetv1
www.youtube.com/user/AllSufficientGod

Amazon
www.amazon.com/author/ndp

Blogger
www.allsufficientgod.blogspot.com

Sow Into This Ministry

The ministry efforts of All Sufficient God Church are funded by donations and financial gifts from people like you. Every year, we see the lives of countless people impacted and transformed. By investing into All Sufficient God Church, you can be excited to know that you are a vital part of this process.

You can make a one-time donation, or become a monthly giver. Your generosity enables us to reach more people with the Good News of Jesus Christ. At the end of the year you will receive a tax-deductible receipt for your tax purposes. Thank you for your generosity and commitment to the Lord!

To sow a financial seed, please visit: www.AllSufficientGod.org/give.php

Schedule Nathan D. Pietsch

If you desire to schedule Nathan D. Pietsch for a speaking engagement you can contact All Sufficient God Church at:

www.AllSufficientGod.org

Nathan preaching in Kenya, Africa.

Nathan preaching in Oregon, USA.

Nathan preaching in Nigeria, Africa.

Nathan preaching in Washington, USA.

Forefathers' Blood

By Nathan D. Pietsch

Our forefathers' blood is being disgraced.
It is up to us to not let their sacrifice be erased.

Our forefathers were farmers who became patriots.
They did not anticipate their hopes of freedom spawning hate riots.

Our forefathers fought and died for freedom's sake.
The women watched their loved ones go with deep heartache.

Our forefathers overcame tyranny for America's sake.
They knew such evil must break.

Our forefathers battled against oppression that kept them bound
So yours and my liberty could be found.

Our forefathers fought and died to lose the bonds of wickedness.
They did not see future generations full of fickleness.

Our forefathers shook free of the heavy burden.
They knew they had to obtain victory, that's for certain.

Our forefathers overcame the oppressors to be free.
They had a dream of God's glory spreading from sea to shining sea.

Our forefathers suffered under an overwhelming yoke
To avoid our nation falling to the Ideology of Woke.

Our forefathers envisioned a land of the free and the home of the brave.
Let us not let their vision rot in the grave.

Our forefathers paid a great sacrifice.
To forget their legacy will not suffice.

Our forefathers' blood is crying from the ground,
"Don't lose this liberty we have found!"

Our forefathers fought and died in miry mud.
We must remember our forefathers' blood.

Get Right With God

Jesus is knocking at the door of your heart. He wants to empower, heal, deliver, and save you. If you desire to answer the call of Jesus and step into your true God-given destiny, please say the following prayer with sincerity of heart.

Jesus said, "Follow Me."

"Lord, I know that I have broken Your laws and commandments. I know I have fallen short of Your perfection. I am a sinner and in need of a Savior. Please forgive me of all my sins. Wash me clean in the blood of Jesus. I invite Jesus to become my Lord and Savior, to rule and reign in my heart from this day forward. Please baptize me with the Holy Spirit and fire. I receive all that You have for me. I pray all of this in the name of Jesus. Amen."

If this is the first time you have ever said this prayer, I want to welcome you into the family of God. You can now begin to fully experience the joy, peace, love, and power of the Heavenly Father, Jesus Christ, and Holy Spirit. We would love to hear from you and support you in your journey.

www.ingramcontent.com/pod-product-compliance
Lightning Source LLC
Chambersburg PA
CBHW072049290426
44110CB00014B/1607